Almosts

by
Kennedy Scott

Dedications:

To Zee: This book truly would not exist without you and your friendship. Thank you for pushing me to pursue courage over comfort. You have helped inspire the healing of so much hurt you never caused. Truly one of the brightest lights I've ever experienced in this world. I have so much love and respect for you.

To my Mama: Thank you for teaching me it's okay to fall down and get hurt sometimes; as long as I get back up.
I love you dearly

To Granny Nora: You have always loved me with such a genuine and healing wholeness. I would not be the person I am today without you.
I love you with my entire heart.

Authors Note:

I wrote this book in an effort to heal and push my own boundaries of comfort.
I started this book in complete interpersonal disarray. But I feel in the time writing it I have found not only closure but a new sense of strength, individuality, and growth.
To all those struggling with their almosts, know that they don't define you, your worth, or your character.
Thank you to everyone who contributed to an almost in my life: it has allowed me to finish the story with growth and opportunity.
Integrity goes beyond the words we say. Integrity lies in our character and the ways in which we decide to respond to situations that challenge our perception of ourselves.
-Kennedy

Table Of Contents

Almosts

Nothing has burned
quite like a string of almosts

The so close's
the embraces that mean *some*thing
because It wasn't nothing
and then you realized i'm not *your* thing

A heart of a hopeless romantic
the type that sees a love story in small moments
poetry in the trees
and love in the sunsets

Tell me your favorite part of your day
let me see the glimmer in your eye
and the pitch change in your voice
tell me what makes your soul feel at peace
you have no idea how good you look
when your face lights up

My softness is attractive until it becomes a dealbreaker
It's not a first impression
it doesn't go away
It's not a facade
It's me -
firm in my vulnerability

I'm stuck in a cycle
a stream of messages
Don't rush - It'll come:
The picket fence
The I do's
The ever afters

But I always end up with
More than friends
Sorta lovers
But only for a moment
An almost

While a moments beauty can last a life
Time is short and love is sweet
But the goodbyes are always so bitter

It's like losing a pack -
before getting to your lucky cigarette
Using your last roll of film -
to never get it developed
Being so close to making it
Only to miss the part I was looking forward to the most
Isn't that ironic
A cliffhanger
Always stuck in limbo

I cant remember how your hand felt in mine
It's been long enough
I don't feel it anymore
But I do recall how the light hit your eye
The inflection in your laugh
And the way you looked at me
Because we *almost* made it
We were so close
It wasn't nothing
We were something
And regardless

I am still somebody
always me
always soft
always here
-K.S.

ATW

It's just a song
10 minutes and 13 seconds
Love found and love lost
A bridge we crossed
A chorus we sang
But nothing gets stuck in my head
Quite like the thought of you

-K.S.

Green Light

We had the green light
so I hit the gas
and you slammed on the brakes

A limbo

With the engine revving
we ran out of fuel

So you got out
and walked away
saying it was for help
but you never looked back

but I saw the way you glanced at me
for a moment
when the light turned green

And for just one moment
with an open road
and no care for a destination
as long as it was us
we were ready to go

-K.S.

I Miss You

I miss you -
but I'll be okay

I wish it would've been you -
but I've accepted it will be someone else

I want the magic moments
the late nights
the early mornings
the "I'm home safe's"
and the "I miss you's"
in the middle of the workday

But

I don't want to seem too desperate
I want to show intention
but
I don't want to come off too eager

I'll find it with someone else
the time will come and it will feel right
it will be new
it will be magic

It won't be you
I'll forget that's what I even wanted
but for the moment

I miss you
I miss the idea of us
I miss the hope of we
but it will be someone else
even if it's just me

-K.S.

If It Wasn't Love

If it wasn't love -
tell me what was sitting in your eyes
when you looked at me
at a red light
under the stars
or in the bedroom
at my parents house

If it wasn't love -
tell me why it's so hard to forget
tell me I was the only one
tell me you're a liar

If it wasn't love -
tell me what was behind every kiss we shared
gasping for breath
clenching the bed sheets
telling me softly - "I feel safe"

If it wasn't love -
tell me what was behind
sharing your favorite music
tell me what you meant
when you asked if I made it home safe
or if I felt okay after a long night

If it wasn't love -
tell me why
there was a glimmer in your eye
every time
you talked about the idea of us

It was love -
it's not forever
it won't be
but for the rest of my life
I'll wonder
what if?

    -K.S.

Sweeter Goodbyes

I always long for a sweeter goodbye
some sort of explanation
a reason

Why the magic wasn't enough
Why the love wasn't enough
Why *I* wasn't enough

-K.S.

Sometimes a Muse

Sometimes a muse
goes beyond the words on a page

Sometimes a muse
means you drop your vices
the smoking
the drinking
the self-deprecation

Sometimes a muse
inspires a smile
a laugh
or a string of tears

Sometimes a muse
is the reason to flip the record
to change the light bulb
to keep going

Sometimes the muse only stays on the page
I have my words
I have the pages
but I'll never have you

-K.S.

If You Have To Leave

If you have to leave
all I ask
is please don't forget me

If you have to leave
don't forget the hope you once held
of the idea for us

If you have to leave
don't forget the laughs we shared
the chorus' we sang
the nights we held one another

If you have to leave
don't forget
there was once a time
where the thought of me
was enough
                    -K.S.

The Love Story

I want the love story
but I don't need the roses
I just want the love story
that ends in you and me together
because every time we lock eyes
or share a smile
or lean in for a kiss
no words could ever add up
to how I feel about you
-K.S.

Would You Still Love Me?

In a day where we hear
"would you still love me if…"
as if love was that conditional

as if somehow
we could wrap the complexities of us
into a simple being
like a worm

But I need to know -
would you still love me if I was just me?
would you love my bad days
my off days
when I'm ugly crying
or when I miss you

Would you still love me
if you had every option in the world
every beautiful creature you could imagine
and you had to seek me out

Would you still love me
if I hadn't said it first
if I hadn't bought the flowers
or if I hadn't leaned in for the first kiss

Would you still love me
if it wasn't so convenient
if I wasn't right in front of you
if there were miles between us
and odds stacked against us -
would you still choose me?

Would you still love me
if all I had to offer
was me
        -K.S.

"Yes…"

I asked if you had fell for me
you said
"yes

.

.

.

but"

and that's all I needed to know

-K.S.

The Right Thing

I know the right thing
would be to move on
and to forget
what we were
what we did
how we felt

I know the right thing
would be to lose the hope
that someday you'll come around
we'll meet again
and maybe you'll remember
what we could be

I know the right thing
would be to delete your number
not ask how you're doing
to just keep walking

But the idea of taking first steps
and moving past what we had
feels so wrong
when everything between us
always felt so right

-K.S.

My Getaway

Music was always my happy place
my getaway
the only thing to quiet my mind

until I met you
and the desire to run
slowly melted away
-K.S.

My Heart Breaks

My heart breaks for you
always on the run
never able to trust love

My heart breaks for you
never able to commit
not to anyone else
or to what you really want

My heart breaks for you
almost more than mine broke
the day you walked away

-K.S.

Pieces

I am not the same person today
as I was before you
just as I wasn't the same person
after meeting anyone who's crossed my path

for better or for worse I take a bit
of every single person who touches my life
just as I give up a piece of myself
a piece of my heart
to each of those I love

a never-ending roundabout of new tastes
music
food
the way I love
the way I want love

I never see things in the same light
influence is a never-ending reminder
of lost connections
missed relationships
and bittersweet endings

But you, darling, are in everything
a refreshment of my senses
everything looked different

What was once a refreshing taste of something new
now makes every encounter
taste like it's laced in lemon juice
a sourness I wasn't prepared for
so I choose to listen
to the songs we've listened to
a million times
like it's the first time
and like you're still mine

-K.S.

Soft

You always framed my vulnerability
as a weakness more than a strength
initially refreshing
but impossible to thrive
in an environment of toxic

Consistent vulnerability
went from a breath of fresh air
into
"is this how you always are"
a constant reminder
I don't act as I should
"how can you look so tough
and show up so gentle"

With repetition you assured
I'd know to hide it
to hold it in
to show *enough*
but not *too much*

But without my soft edges
there is no me
strength over a weakness
a sign of courage to be honest

My greatest strength
is holding on to me
a softness that can not be displaced
a boldness to be true
A passion to stay soft
in a world that wants so badly
for me to be hardened

Because of you
and despite you,
I *am* harder than before
harder to crack
harder to break
and it's so much harder
to make me question if I am the right thing

What's not right for you
is right for me
                    -K.S.

Touch

I can't remember how you feel
not because
we haven't touched
but because
you aren't the person I once knew

-K.S.

Missed Calls

Every morning I wake up
hoping for
a missed call
a missed text
some sort of sign that
I crossed your mind

-K.S.

O.C.D.

There is a certain calculation
that helps me thrive
rooted in obsessive compulsion
a focus on details
a desire to have everything be right

A good list
a set of instructions
anything that tells me I did something correct

But moving on
doesn't come with a rulebook
there's no recipe for being okay

there are no instructions
to forget how your lips felt on mine
or how good it was
to hear you say my name
or even sweeter
call me yours

I want so badly to feel right
in moving on from you
getting over you
forgetting what we had

How is this supposed to feel right
when nothing has ever clicked like you -
nothing has ever tasted sweeter
than the idea of you and me

There isn't a lot of room
for rightness in feeling -
it's subjective
interpretive
open

I have always been stuck in the mind
that stresses every little detail
but you brought a serene peace
a certain quietness
that always felt just right

                    -K.S.

Enough

I sometimes wonder
why I'm not quite enough
when I give
more than my all

How is love
not quite enough
what scale are we using
to grade the efficacy -
a whole person
but not quite enough

if I give up every bit of me
and it's not quite enough
what does that say about me
when will I be enough?
                          -K.S.

Hooked

An addictive personality -
first a hurricane
of booze and broads
pills and parties
a delicious cocktail of dopamine
a rush like no other

I put down the bottle
it wasn't impossible to quit
watching the days tick by
hundreds and counting

It was never the body -
as soft as your skin was
as sweet as your touch was
as intoxicating as the sound of your voice
drunk on you for nights to come
the sweetest relief

You, my dear
were never that easy
the greatest high
the sweetest buzz
the softest brew
and the toughest to quit

You, my dear
were different
with you
my dear
it was love
and that was my biggest addiction of all

-K.S.

Cigarettes Under the Moonlight

Open a pack
flip the lucky
you ask me why I chose *that* one
call me superstitious
call it tradition
but I think it may be fate

Light it up
yours first
mine second
always making sure you're set

The first inhale
never thought it was that indulgent
but with you next to me
under the moonlight,
there was nothing that could have tasted better

A subtle shiver
on a cool night
but you grab the outline of my face
pull me in
and kiss me

calm

Was it nerves?
did I just need the warmth of your touch?
or was it just connection?
- *I think it may be fate*

Subtle talks
music
family
goals
us
but none of the words are sticking
all I focus on is the warmth
the warmth of you
the warmth of the hope of us

Halfway through
as the ash falls -
the temperature drops
but I feel warm and cozy
like a fire on Christmas eve
nothing feels more like home
than the thought of you

A final puff
a final flick
the promise of the rest of the pack
ours
something we share

What a drag it was
to fall for you
to open a pack
for it to never be finished
we never got our lucky
but I guess that's why we save it for last
you made such a short time
feel like forever
you made such a short time
feel like fate

I was never much for cigarettes
but if they're with you
I'd spend the rest of my days smoking
a feeling I long for
the promise of a pack
never finished
only forgotten
but I think, that too
may be fate
                    -K.S.

You Haven't Passed

Sometimes
I pretend like you've passed away
because it's easier to process
the loss of you
in definite terms
in the idea that there is no you

I see love through a lens -
always with me
but "in memory of"
feels easier than
"what could've been"

I act like you aren't only an hour away
if I pretend there are a million miles
between you and I
the distance seems far greater
than the distance you created
after you looked at me with love
and you told me you fell
just to turn around and walk away

it is easier for me to believe
there's no transportation
that could get me to you
than the idea that you'd want to let us go

You're still here
but you passed
on
the chance we had
the science between us
the love in our eyes
and the softness of our touch

You haven't died
but sometimes I think
it would be easier if you did
because how can we live on this earth
with a connection like ours
and not find a way

It would be easier
because if you were gone
it would mean
I was enough
                    -K.S.

Addiction

Addiction never tasted as sweet as you
but when you ran out of juice
I was only left with a bottle
of broken promises
numbed feelings
drunk texts and
countless regrets

It was never a problem
until we were no more
the liquor was endless -
an easier drowning
than the thought of losing you

When the bottle ran out
and rock bottom was met
I was able to feel
I was able to grow
I was able to forget you
and the hold you had
on my ability to swim

After sober nights
it was difficult to tell
which was the worse hell
missing you or missing the bottle

But the bottle was just a substitute
a drink here
a pill there
the real addiction was always you

I am addicted to the idea
that maybe someday I'll get a call
I'm addicted to wondering
if it was something I did
I'm addicted to wondering
if it was something I didn't do
I'm addicted to wanting to know if I was
the only one
who felt what we had
who felt us

Six months sober
I don't think about the bottle anymore
no longer trying to self medicate
with a sea of intoxication

Six months sober
but still trying to figure out
how to kick the habit of you

-K.S.

Happy Without You

You always said
I'd be happy without you
a truth I never believed
until it came to fruition

The years passed
always with tunnel vision
one desire - never changing
it was always you

The closer we were
the clearer it was
"how *could* I be
happy without you"

I fell and I tried
you burned me a few too many times
always dying to hear you say
"I'm happy with you"

But as you use
and throw away
people you say you love
the question changed
"how could I be
happy *with* you"

Instant gratification comes at a price
as you flip through sapphics
like the Uno cards you hold so dear
always questioning
"why can't I keep one near"

A cycle doesn't end
when the behavior
stays a trend
you care more about bedpost notches
than you do keeping a friend

You always said
"you'll be happy without me"
but the answer is
I am happiest with *me*
a truth that isn't exclusive
a truth that isn't dependent
on you

I couldn't have found me
without the pain of you
and I hope others know themselves well enough
to avoid suffering through
the havoc you wreak
hopefully the next one
can make it more than a week

As you continue to lead people on
including yourself
instilling a false hope
a false sense of confidence
that you'll stick around
I hope you look inwards
and ask yourself
"am I happy with me"

-K.S.

If I Ever Leave Too Soon

If I ever leave too soon
please know it was nobody's fault
it wasn't with malice
it wasn't to make anyone cry
it was just my time
even if it felt too early

If I ever leave too soon
please know I gave all I had
I went until my cup ran out
I gave too much
took too little
but never regretted a moment

If I ever leave too soon
don't say there were signs
or there's more you should've done
my purpose has always been to love
and if I leave too soon
know that I fulfilled my purpose
to give all I had
until there was no more

If I ever leave too soon
know that I love you

-

Focus on the laughter
sing a song in my honor
love as I would have
remember the purpose

If I ever leave too soon
I'm okay with it
and I want you to be too

-K.S.

Lonely Smoker

A cigarette without you
just tastes like a cigarette
but I'll keep inhaling
in hopes it somehow
brings me closer to you

-K.S

Lie To Me

I always pride myself on integrity
and holding others to the same standard
but late at night
when I'm most alone
I wish you would just lie to me

Lie to me
and tell me you miss me
tell me I was important to you
tell me you think of me when you're alone
tell me what we had was special

Lie to me
give me any sign I didn't waste my time
give me a reason to believe what we had was honest
let me know that you want me back
even if you have to

Lie to me
because accepting dishonesty
is easier than accepting the truth
if the truth is that you didn't care
we weren't special - at least not to you
Please,
Lie to me

       -K.S.

Is It Wrong

We never dated
never made anything official
so I need to know
is it wrong for me to miss you

Stuck between a situation
and a friendship
we hung out every day
told each other everything
so I need to know
is it wrong for me to want more

You wanted to work on yourself
we all need growth
I am no exception
I don't want to impede
in a journey of improvement
so I need to know
is it wrong for me to think I could help

You shared your favorite music
and it slowly became mine
I still play it - thinking of you, thinking of us
I feel so proud when I memorize another bridge
so I need to know
is it wrong for me to want to tell you

Is it wrong for me to remember
the nights we shared together
skin on skin
lingering in that feeling
drowning in the thought of you
wanting to feel *us* again

Maybe I'm stubborn
maybe I'm stupid
maybe I'm wrong
sitting here and wondering
what if we tried
what if we faced the fear of falling

It might be wrong
but I think
we could have made it

                    -K.S.

The White Hat

Comfort in discomfort
a foundation of trust and safety
as you grab me and tell me "It's okay"

A look in my eye
as you let me take the lead
with every past encounter
etched into the gentle embrace
a responsibility
as you ask me to hold your favorite white hat

The soft gentleness
as the hat is placed in my hands
a memento you've had your whole life
carefully protected
always valued, always secure
a responsibility I take with the weight
of those you came close to trusting before

Intentional protection
a comfort in the warmth of the hat
now substituted with us
calmly asking if the comfort it provides
is adequately addressed
and sufficiently replaced

A foreward of importance
a foreshadowing of leaving
the person trusted
would hold on to it
long after you depart

I still reminisce
how you looked as you handed it to me
putting your trust
in the gentleness of my approach
but you left
and as I keep the hat with me
I wish I still had you
instead of just the memory
of the night
you left me
your favorite white hat

-K.S.

Fighting Myself

Every single day
I wake up
and go to sleep
fighting myself
and the urge to tell you
I miss you

-K.S.

I Stayed

I stayed
despite being given every reason not to
because even though your actions
told me to run for the hills
there was a moment I thought I'd run away with you
maybe I was reminiscent of the few good moments
or maybe it was when you asked me
to meet you at the courthouse
and let you know I was yours

I came back
because even though you showed me
the ease of my disposal
there was once a moment
where you made me feel the safest
to exist without expectation
and to show up without a veil of preservation

I defended
despite you making it seem like I was never there
never what you wanted and only a placeholder
disregarding what felt like a lifetime
of "You're what I've been looking for"
only to turn around - months later
and tell me you defended me publicly
so our shame was only private

I left
because after more time fighting you
than the time I got to love you
I learned
that you only want a momentary infatuation
a temporary obsession
just long enough for an Instagram highlight
because something as vulnerable
as commitment and intention
would require you to be honest
and you were never much of a fan
of telling the truth

-K.S.

First Impressions

A first impression
is more than just a moment
it's a lasting mark
a tone-setting decision-maker
on who I am
and who I will be

If I was all my first impression
to you I'd be ever nervous
with a shaking grip
a soft embrace
a nervous giggle and
an avoidant gaze

But perhaps that is who I am
always much softer
than people expect
a specific gentleness
when anticipation reads harshness

My first impression reads unsure
of myself
or what I want and what I'm capable of
but it couldn't be further from me
because if first impressions were true
I'd be sure we're meant to be

First impressions can be telling
and maybe you should read more into it
the soft nervousness
isn't that far from the truth
but there's also conviction and strength -
it's needed really
being soft in a world that is so rough
a strength needed
to go against the grain
to go against expectation
and to stay true to me
over what you may want me to be

-K.S.

Passing By

I sometimes like to think of us
like the sun and the moon

Every single time
they pass each other by
a beautiful explosion of color
paints everybody's sky

but as the moon lives in a dark expanse
hoping for a little bit of light
all the sun wants is to retreat
to have a moment of quiet

Maybe it's not their time
as they keep passing each other by
day in and day out
however close they may feel
they'll never be together

My darling sunshine
however many times we may pass each other by
as I see the portrait we paint
each time we get close
I thank you

As I get lost in my darkness
I know at the end of the long night
I get a moment of hope
a small glimpse of you
and if passing each other by
looks that good
imagine what we could paint
if we ever made it

-K.S.

Promises

I promised you
I'd always be here
I'd never go
regardless of context
regardless of subject

Promises made
not realizing
cheering you on
may mean cheering on
the other girl

It's not dishonest
my faith in you
my consistency
my presence
it's not untruthful
because I promised

Promises only mean as much
as the integrity the sender holds
and despite you not keeping yours
I refuse to lose mine
I promise

So I will continue to root for you
even from afar
because I told you I'd always be here
and through blocked numbers
and missing texts
I still wish you well

As much as it may hurt
when you root on my downfall
I can't wait to see you
as I wish you to grow up
because I promised
and I hope someday
you remember
and you regret
what you promised me

-K.S.

Expectations

You left saying
"I can't give you what you need"
but the worst part is
you are all I need

-K.S.

Playlists

I made you a playlist
updated every single day
but you never saw it
I never shared the link

I made you a playlist
The melodies are reminders
of what we could've been
of time spent together
and how we felt back then

I made you a playlist
but deleted it one day
as you told me we'd be better
if we ended it as friends

I made you a playlist
I still have all the songs
but it all feels so silly
not that you've moved on

I made you a playlist
of feelings in the moment
one day hoping
we'd be listening together

-K.S.

Every Notification

Every notification
is the shortest poem ever written
hope and heartbreak
in a matter of seconds
because every time I check
it's never you

                -K.S.

10 Minutes

What I wouldn't give
for just 10 minutes
inside your head
to know exactly how you feel
to know what you think of
when you think of me
if you think of me

What I would do
for just 10 minutes
10 more minutes with you
in the time where you looked at me
with a sparkle in your eye
like you were happy to be with me

What a difference
10 minutes can make
in that short time
I went from thinking I was yours
to saying goodbye
all in a matter
of 10 minutes

                 -K.S.

For You

Since our debut,
I was always fearless
and you let it get the best of you

All I wanted was for you to speak
now and then
tell me how you feel

But as our tide turned red
we lost contact
89 reasons not to reach out
a hell of a reputation to get over

But then

I saw you again
and from first sight
all I wanted
was to make you my lover

Odds stacked against us forever
more so than before
because this time it was real
this time we approached it
sharing midnights together

One simple connection
one common denominator
what we had was real
never folklore
we had our redo
it was our version
we just didn't let it play out

I miss you
            -K.S.

Moving On

Moving on -
something I've been waiting for
as I would sit and cry
wondering why it didn't work
my only wish was - moving on

It's happened now
I still think about you
but without the heavy grief
without the longing
without the feeling of missing something
larger than us both

Moving on
now feels so wrong
I feel guilt for letting you go
as if I owed you something
a forever
but that's what I promised

I'll wait for your call
and keep the door unlocked
because realistically
you'll always have
a home with me

                -K.S.

Moments

Sometimes love
isn't forever
it's not a lifetime
not even a long time
sometimes- it's just a moment

I look back
at a compilation of moments
enough to make a movie
and by far the sweetest
were with you

There will be moments with others
a hope for something greater
but in those moments
I hope it circles back to you

Perhaps we were meant to be
if only for a moment
to cross paths
and find the sweetest embrace
even when time came to let go
and our moment came to an end
I will continue to hold on to the softness
the hope of holding you
for longer than a moment

If you ever decide to come back
and see if we can turn a moment
into the chance for forever
I will welcome you with open arms
an eagerness to love
but with just a soft hesitation
of losing another moment

If you ever decide to come back
for one more moment
I won't question why
or for how long
as long as I can get
one more moment
                    -K.S.

Coincidences

I wouldn't call it love
more of a coincidence

It's not that I loved you
I just kept a note of fun facts
your favorite things
your least favorite things
just in case anybody ever asks
in case anybody needs to know you

I wouldn't call it love
but you can have my last 10 dollars
you can have my free time
I'll give you my attention
and a little reserve in my heart
but that's just a coincidence

It doesn't have to be love
we were never official
just an almost
an in between
the feelings are present
but commitments not required
more of a same place
same time
a coincidence

We don't have to say love
but it was there
we can call it whatever you want
as long as the story we read
is one that involves you and I
I don't believe in destiny
but I do believe in coincidences
and we were the most beautiful of all

-K.S.

Let Go

It's hard to let go
not just of the moments we shared
or the nights we spent together
the car rides
with our favorite songs
and moments to glance over

But it's hard to let go
of the feeling in my stomach
when I would smell your perfume
a feeling familiar to that of being home
a comfort and excitement
a calm rollercoaster
filled with desire

It's hard to let go of the warmth I felt
battling against the cold december night
as I grab your face
and lean in for a kiss
getting lost in that feeling
wanting it to last forever
hoping
that when you leave
I can conjure up the nerve
to tell you I miss that

It's hard to let go of the hope
something beyond a connection
a feeling deep in my heart
that moves me to get up each day
a desire to get better
to be better
to be everything you could want

It's hard to let go
of the idea that maybe
just maybe
we were the right people
and it was the wrong time
and someday
you might wake up
and realize it's our time

-K.S.

Tell Me

If it was just you and I
with no one else around
no expectations
no commitments
no requirements

Would you tell me
that you miss me
that you want me
that you fucked up
that you want to try again?

-K.S.

Be Kind in Your Goodbyes

Be as kind in your goodbye as you are
in your hello's
in your I love you's
in your "this made me think of you"
in the way you hold me
in the way you tell me I'm yours

Be as kind in your goodbyes as you are
when you tell me I'm safe to relax
hands running through my hair
not having to worry about
the feeling of being perfect

Be as soft in your goodbye as you were
with our first kiss
or the first time you laid your head on my chest
whispering "this means something"

Be kind in your goodbyes
because my heart cant take many more

Be kind in your goodbyes
or please don't say hello

-K.S.

Growth

Growth is never linear
if anything it's more of
a back and forth
with your hands on 10 and 2
a few extra turns
but we all get there

Sometimes in growth
we have to put ourselves
in the past -
the past feelings
the past experiences
the past truths
because even if we may not feel them now
they still have a hold
until we've read the chapter
and closed the book

In the effort of growth
we have to reevaluate
who's part of the story
who holds us back
and who wants to only exist in past terms
we have to acknowledge
but we can not dwell

Sometimes with growth
we must recognize
that occasionally we leave those behind
who we once thought
were holding us up
helping us reach the finish line
because although we learn
to continue moving
they stay in the spot they've always been
only able to help
for so long

Growth can take many faces
late night tears
words on a page
lyrics to a melody -
but it all takes time
one can not grow
if those around us
don't trust us
when we say we're taking the steps

So I will continue to grow without you
even though you're all I used to want
because I am growing
despite you telling me
it's impossible

-K.S.

The End

The end of you and I
almost came quicker
than the beginning -
a speed and anticipation
of the unexpected
and the unwarranted

The end of you and I
can only come to fruition
if there's trust and belief
that we hold honesty in our word
integrity in our sentiments
and value in our emotion

Resentment is too easy
a burden that bogs us down
in remorse of truths that couldn't be
but at the end of you and me
it's the self-fulfilling prophecy

So I bid you adieu
I wish you well
and as much as I hate to admit it
this is
the end

      -K.S